THE BOOK OF
BOXES

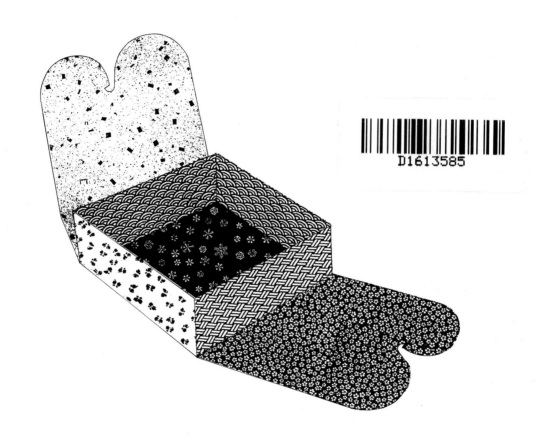

Kunio Ekiguchi

KODANSHA INTERNATIONAL
TOKYO · NEW YORK · LONDON

Photographs by Akihiko Tokue
Line drawings by Toshimasa Terakawa
Schematics by Yasunori Yoshida

Distributed in the United States by Kodansha America, Inc.,
114 Fifth Avenue, New York, N.Y. 10011, and in the United
Kingdom and continental Europe by Kodansha Europe Ltd.,
Gillingham House, 38-44 Gillingham Street, London SW1V
1HU. Published by Kodansha International Ltd., 17-14, Otowa
1-chome, Bunkyo-ku, Tokyo 112, and Kodansha America,
Inc.

ISBN 0-87011-894-3 (USA)
ISBN 4-7700-1394-9 (Japan)

First edition, 1988
93 94 95 10 9 8 7 6

Library of Congress Cataloging-in-Publication Data
Ekiguchi, Kunio, 1930-
The book of boxes.

1. Box making—Japan. I. Title
TT870.5.E55 1988   688.8   88-80136
ISBN 0-87011-894-3 (U.S.)

INTRODUCTION

In shape and material, the Japanese traditional box derives from the art of basketry. Round boxes, square boxes, oblong boxes—boxes that stand up, lie down, twist and fold—bamboo boxes, wooden boxes, *washi* boxes, boxes of beauty and form and style. Their variety is endless, their function basic—to contain, to preserve, to honor items of special significance.

The earliest boxes were used to keep important letters or as a medium for their conveyance. Typically, letters were rolled, placed in an appropriate box, after which the entire box was wrapped in a cloth. Similarly, paintings or calligraphy were mounted on scrolls, rolled, wrapped in crepe paper, then put away for safekeeping in a *washi* box, a box constructed with handmade paper. The same with *kimono*, which were then set into another box made of the softwood of *kiri*, the paulownia tree, then also wrapped in a cloth. Even now, most of the precious accoutrements of tea ceremony are stored in this way. All of these stand as examples of the role of the box in the long and rich tradition of wrapping in Japan.

The practical value of *washi*—which was invented in China in 105 A.D. and its technology brought to Japan in 610—was realized, in particular, by its material strength and its ability to absorb moisture in a humid climate. In Japan *washi* owed much of its strength to the long wood fibers that the papermaking process preserved. This was a technical improvement upon the Chinese original, but it also lent a natural beauty to the paper, in both appearance and texture, that fitted perfectly with the Japanese aesthetic sense.

Washi's original uses were, as might be expected, for the calligraphy of poetry, as popularized by Lady Murasaki's *Tale of Genji*, but *washi* also found its way into Buddhistic ceremony, where it was used to construct the small flowers, dolls, and animals that were placed as totems into funeral caskets. The development of *origami*, the familiar craft of paper folding, was the logical next step. With intricate, ingenious folds, *washi* could be transformed into a crane (or a thousand cranes), a grasshopper, a turtle—even, in recent times, a robot.

Coming in the Nara era, *origami* was soon followed by the evolution of *tsugigami* as an art form—paper collages that combined the disparate components of printing, marbling, dying, gold flaking, as well as a flowing calligraphy—all on the medium of *washi*. These paper collages appeared as pages in lavishly designed books, as decoration, or as artwork in their own right.

In aspects of a complex Japanese etiquette, *washi* likewise became the material of choice. In tea ceremony, for example, *washi* that had been folded and tucked into the breast of a *kimono* was, as part of the ritual, removed to wrap the confection or to wipe the rim of the tea bowl. Thus, the uses of *washi* ranged from the practical to the artistic, from the everyday to the formalized.

The traditional Japanese box was a product of all of the above: the *washi*, the design of the *washi* (in color, texture, print, calligraphy, collage), the folds of *origami*, the applications both practical and special, the presentation of form and aesthetic. Boxes, as noted earlier, appeared in a multitude of shapes and styles to suit various purposes, but in the Heian era there came the introduction of the *tatō*, the envelope or flat-folded case, as a box form. The *tatō* was constructued to lie flat; however, as the envelope was opened, it unfolded into a three-dimensional object. These were no ordinary envelopes, designed as they were to symbolize, say, the plum blossom (and so be a container of petals, a remembrance of a certain springtime) or a star (and so hold a choice piece of jewelry).

The traditional Japanese box, following closely upon the craft of *origami*, also incorporated many *origami* techniques. A single sheet of *washi* was strategically cut, after which mountain and valley folds (folds, as their names indicate, in opposite directions) were cleverly employed to create the desired box. There was, as with *origami*, no need for glue.

In terms of the interior no less than the exterior of the boxes, the pattern design of the *washi* was similar to the aesthetic of *kimono*. With *kimono*, both the inside and the outside patterns were important. One suggested the other, or complemented it, or provided a startling contrast in color or motif. In some cases, there was a slight reveal, as at the neckline or sleeve, a layered effect, to hint at what lay hidden beneath. The variety of boxes reflected these several considerations.

The fourteen boxes contained in this volume draw upon such traditional elements, their uses subject to the tastes of the owner—whether to hold a single flower, some fine chocolates or candies, or a silk scarf. The construction of the boxes, while relying upon mountain folds and valley folds, here has the added touch of influence of Bauhaus paperwork. The colors and patterns are soft, characteristic of a sensibility that prevailed in the Heian era.

Although the notion of a box is common enough, the boxes that you make here will be creations of beauty and style and sentiment. They could, in themselves, be a gift, they could act as a container for a gift, they could—as a expression of your care and handiwork—adorn the home or office. They will be a friend to all.

I would like to take this opportunity to thank Chika Morimura, Toshimasa Terakawa, and Kiyoshi Nishimura, my assistants, for their work on the box designs, and Tomoko Miyashita and Eiko Ikeda for their help with the pattern designs. I also wish to express my appreciation to Michiko Uchiyama and Elmer Luke, my editors at Kodansha International, and Shigeo Katakura and Hideyo Senoh, my designers.

—Kunio Ekiguchi

Tokyo, 1988

General Instructions

In the construction of the traditional Japanese box, there are two basic folds: the mountain fold (such that the effect is a mountain upon the surface of the paper) and the valley fold (in the opposite direction, such that a valley is the effect). Note that these folds are to be performed on the *reverse* pattern (the side on which the pattern covers the entire page), as whether a fold is a mountain or a valley refers to this side of the page.

In the illustrations that follow, the *positive* pattern is represented by the shaded area. Mountain folds are designated by ----------; valley folds by ············.

Once you have cut out the design of the box (an exacto knife or razor blade is best), proceed with the folding. Do all of one kind of fold first, working with a delicate but firm touch, making certain that the folds extend as far as the notation indicates—but no farther.

CELEBRATION BOX

iwaibako

With a plum blossom and bamboo motif taken from a *kimono* design, this box conveys congratulations and good cheer. Within, there is a stylized wave pattern.

SUGGESTED USES: fine chocolates or cookies.

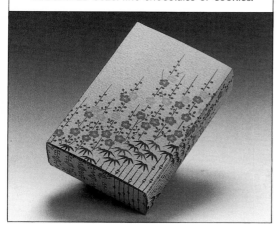

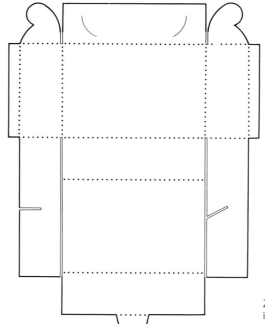

1. The folds completed, bring together the two long flaps. Fix together, left flap over right.

2. Fold the lower edge of the form up, and insert the tabs into their slits. Fold the cover over, and secure with its tab.

PLUM BLOSSOM CASE

umetatō

This flat-folded case symbolizes the flower itself. The patterns, both inside and out, are of various plum blossom motifs.

SUGGESTED USES: a gold chain, a note, petals.

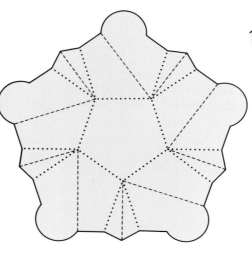

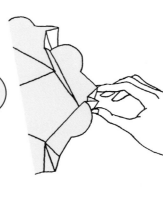

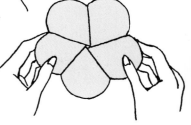

1. Because of its particular design, this box—and this box only—requires that mountain and valley folds be performed on the *positive* pattern. Starting accordingly, press down firmly as you make each mountain and valley fold. This will give the plum blossom its "natural" shape.

2. Enclose the form in both hands, and with your thumbs, arrange the petals of the blossom.

STAR ENVELOPE

hoshitatō

In relief, on the points of this star, is a butterfly pattern. Within is a family crest, also in a butterfly motif.

SUGGESTED USES: spice, potpourri a photo.

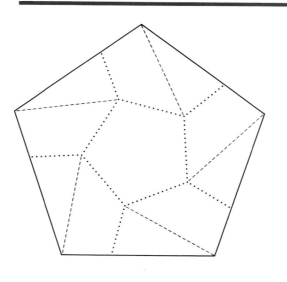

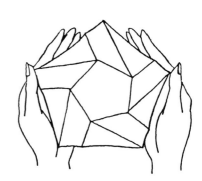

After performing the requisite folds, enclose the star with both hands, allowing the points to fall into place. Twist gently and press firmly, reinforcing the folds.

COTTAGE IN MIDWINTER

ioribako

This snowy scene is rendered with a gold to green cast. Within, the pattern is of stylized snowflakes.

SUGGESTED USES: cosmetics, sweets; perfect for packing a special Christmas gift.

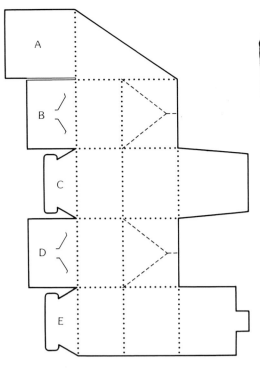

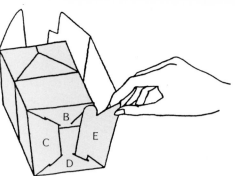

1. The left side of the form constitutes the bottom of this box. After the mountains and valleys have been done, fold in Flap A, followed by B, D, C, and E. Insert the tabs into the slits.

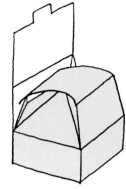

2. As with a milk carton, push in the sides of the top, then slide in the large square flap. Finish the box with the other flap, inserting the tab into the slit.

CANISTER WITH A TWIST

hineribako

A stone pavement pattern, *ishidatami*, is evoked here. Interspersed among the "stones" are the traditional motifs of lattice-work, the chrysanthemum, the morning glory, waves. This exterior is complemented by a smaller, simpler checkerboard pattern.

SUGGESTED USES: perfume, eau de toilette, cosmetics.

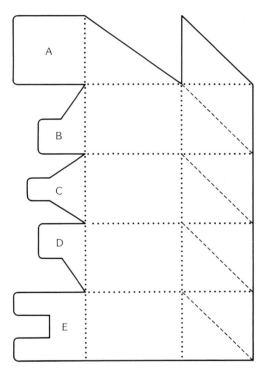

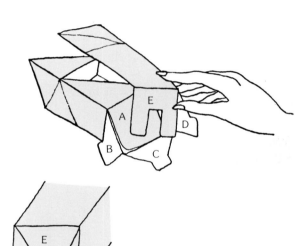

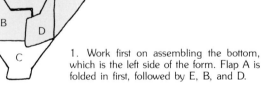

1. Work first on assembling the bottom, which is the left side of the form. Flap A is folded in first, followed by E, B, and D.

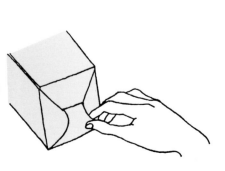

2. Insert Flap C into the slit to secure the bottom.

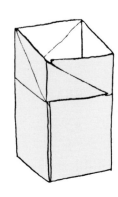

3. Stand the canister upright, with the triangular flap out.

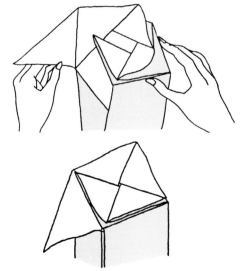

4. Holding the folds at each corner together firmly (two hands are essential), proceed to twist in a clockwise motion so that the twist top appears to rotate on an axis.

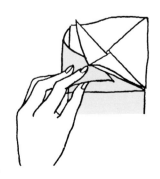

5. Fold the triangular flap over the adjacent lip, and insert under the twist top.

BOX OF WHIRLS

tomoebako

Here is a variation on a theme of a comma-shaped family crest. The autumn grasses on the exterior of the box give the effect of *maki-e*, gold lacquer, with the interior a stylized eddying wave pattern.

SUGGESTED USES: jewelry, cosmetics, elegant accessories.

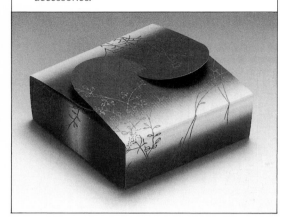

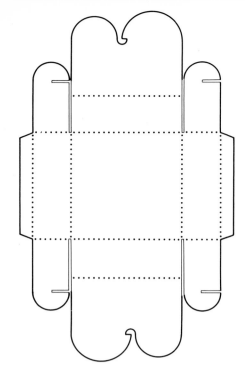

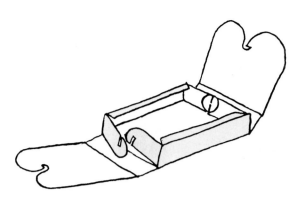

Only valley folds are required here. That done, hold the form vertically in both hands and fit each pair of long tabs together. Finish the box by bringing the large cover flaps together.

HEXAGONAL BOX

rokkakubako

This box is designed to stand vertically. Royal purple stripes alternate with a wisteria vine and flowing branches of two varieties of cherry blossoms. The interior is a variation of the sprinkle effect of gold pellets.

SUGGESTED USES: cookies, biscuits, wrapped candies.

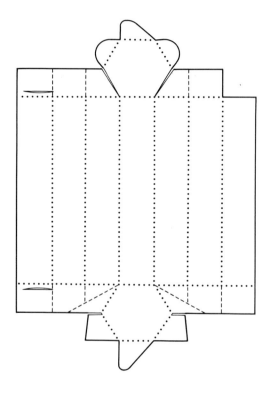

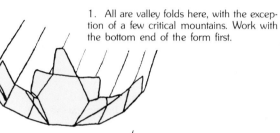

1. All are valley folds here, with the exception of a few critical mountains. Work with the bottom end of the form first.

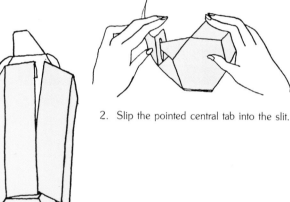

2. Slip the pointed central tab into the slit.

3. Slide the right edge into its channel. Secure the top of the box by inserting the tab into its slit.

TRADITIONAL LETTER BOX

fumibako

Important letters or documents, rolled, were the original purpose of this box. The exterior shows, amid flecks of gold, cranes in flight; the interior is a pattern of clouds.

SUGGESTED USES: a letter of love, a single rose.

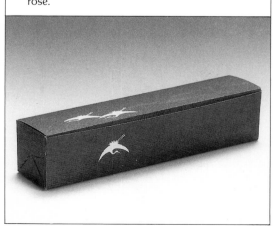

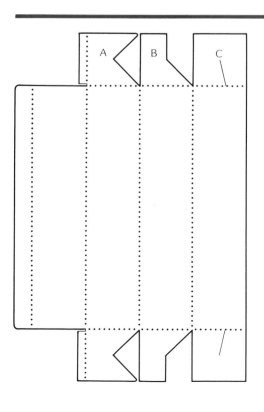

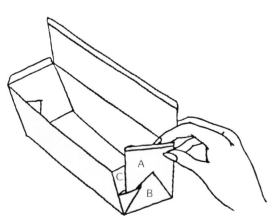

There are only valley folds here. That done, hold the form at one end, and fold the flaps in order: Flap C first, then B, then A. Insert the point of Flap A into the slit of Flap C. Do the same for the other end of the box; finish by tucking the long flap into the box.

TRIANGULAR PRISM

kinchakubako

The mountains pictured on this box were originally rendered by the technique of *kindei*, gold dusting. Within, the moon and pine tree landscape, a scene from a Noh songbook, was evoked by ink marbling, *suminagashi*.

SUGGESTED USES: jewelry, such as earrings, a pin, a brooch.

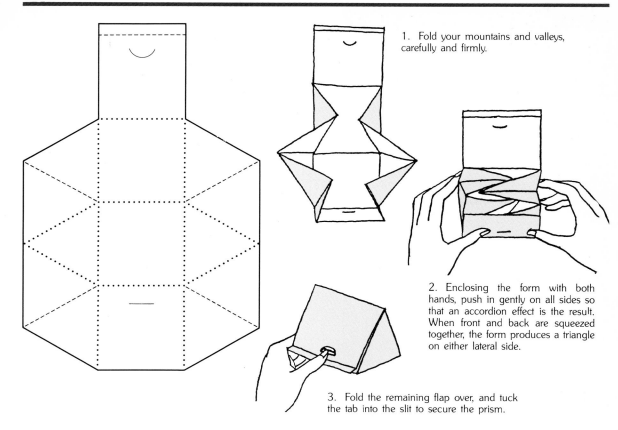

1. Fold your mountains and valleys, carefully and firmly.

2. Enclosing the form with both hands, push in gently on all sides so that an accordion effect is the result. When front and back are squeezed together, the form produces a triangle on either lateral side.

3. Fold the remaining flap over, and tuck the tab into the slit to secure the prism.

BOX WITH A TUCK

sashikomibako

This box relies upon the tuck, an element common in Japanese boxes, for its final touch. Both the exterior and interior derive from traditional *kimono* patterns.

SUGGESTED USES: accessories, a handkerchief, a scarf.

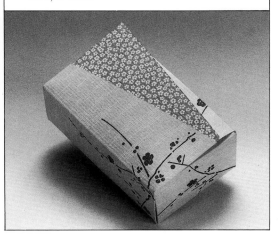

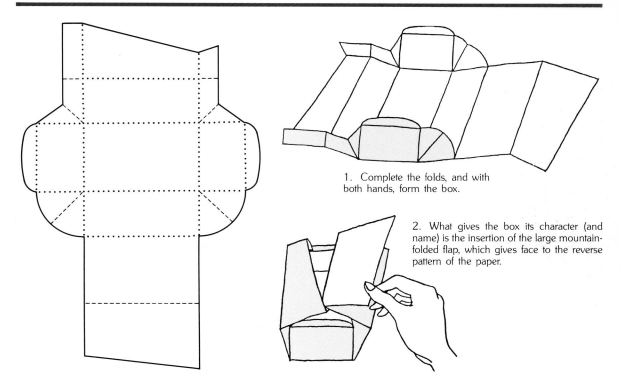

1. Complete the folds, and with both hands, form the box.

2. What gives the box its character (and name) is the insertion of the large mountain-folded flap, which gives face to the reverse pattern of the paper.

MOON BOX

tsukimibako

A silver moon rises over the Chinese bellflower. Within the box is the well-known verse by the Heian poet Kino Tsurayuki, from *The Anthologies of the Thirty-six Poets, Sanjūrokunin kashū*.

SUGGESTED USES: a silk scarf, a linen handkerchief.

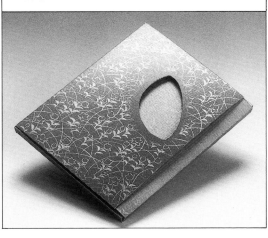

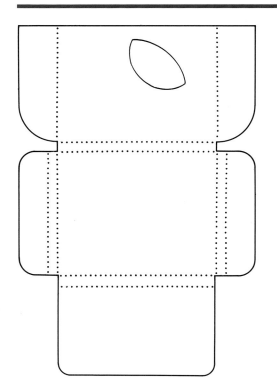

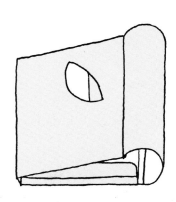

Complete the folds, and insert the large flap into the pocket.

CHRYSANTHEMUM BOX

kikuoribako

In this rendering of the classic Japanese flower, the exterior offers a hint of pampas grass, *susuki*. The interior completes the autumn imagery with a stenciling of the Japanese maple leaf, *momiji*.

SUGGESTED USES: accessories, a ring, a watch, a bracelet, though so virtuoso a box as this could stand alone.

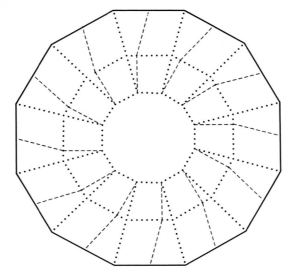

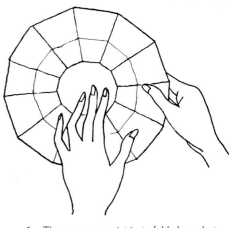

1. There are many intricate folds here, but correctly done, they hold the key to this complex construction. Work from the center of the circle and proceed with the folds concentrically.

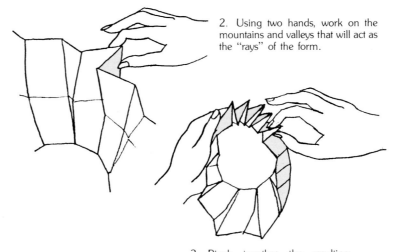

2. Using two hands, work on the mountains and valleys that will act as the "rays" of the form.

3. Pinch together the resulting edges, and work your way around the flower to form the petals.

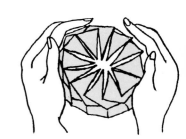

4. Using both hands again, round out the flower.

GENJI BOXES

Genjibako

These boxes portray an aesthetic that prevailed in the Heian era, the time in which *The Tale of Genji* takes place. The elaborate exterior is reminiscent of the bold designs, dusted with silver, that were introduced in *The Anthologies of the Thirty-six Poets, Sanjūrokunin kashū*, published in the early 11th century. It is set off by an unadorned interior.

SUGGESTED USES: The two boxes can be used alone, as a tray or open container, or together, to form a whole—for small precious items, rings, mementos, or practical items such as dressing table necessities.

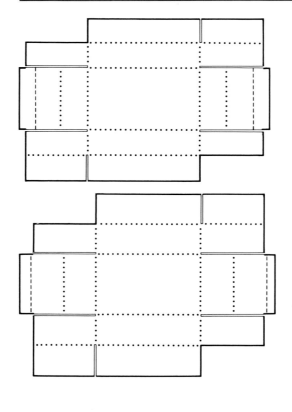

1. The preliminary folds completed, fold in the long flaps on both sides of the middle portion of the form.

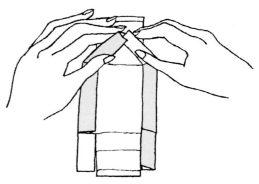

2. At one end of the form, slip the flap into its corresponding channel.

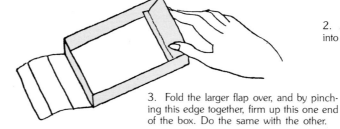

3. Fold the larger flap over, and by pinching this edge together, firm up this one end of the box. Do the same with the other.

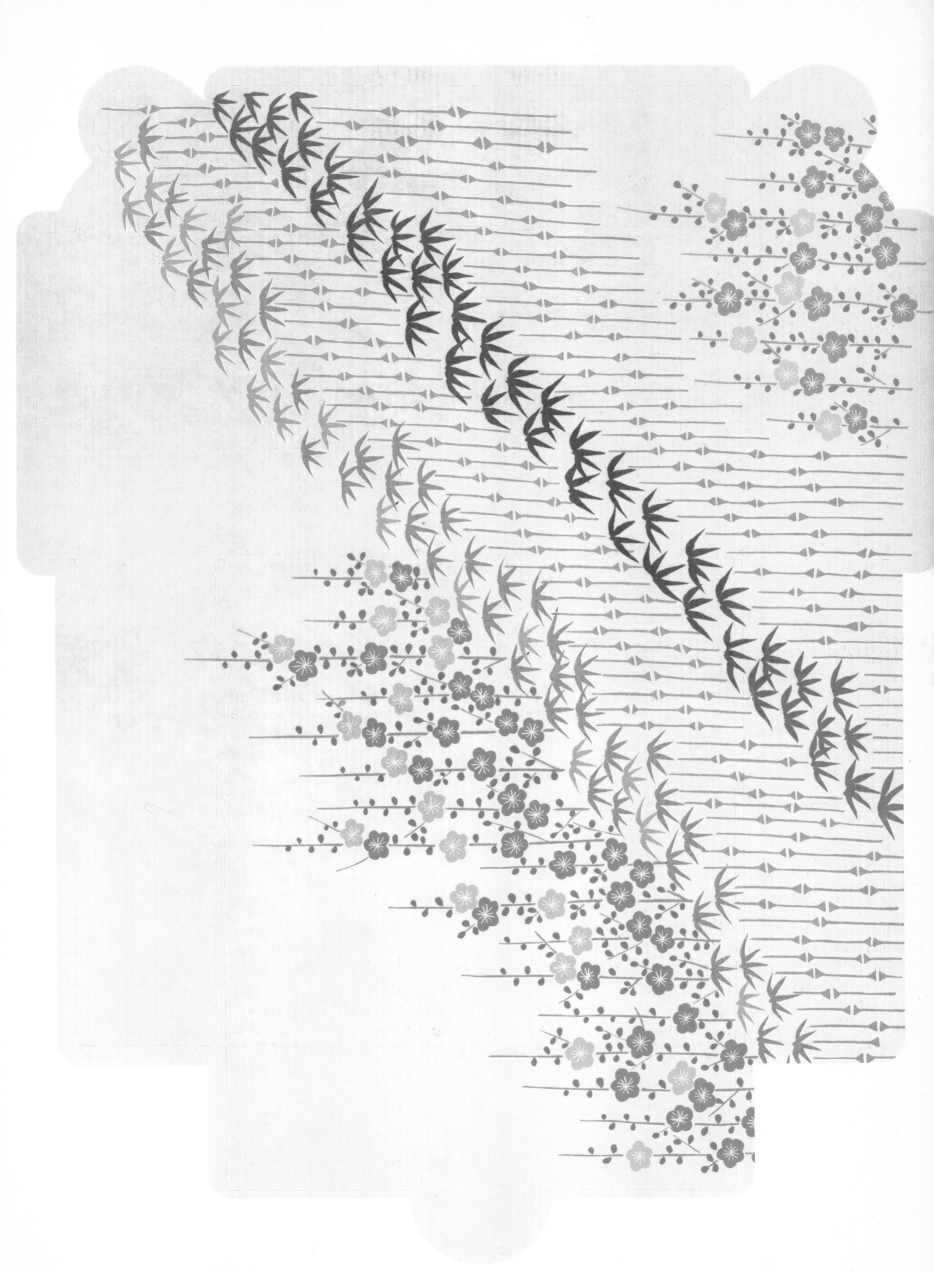

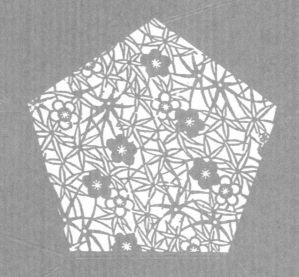

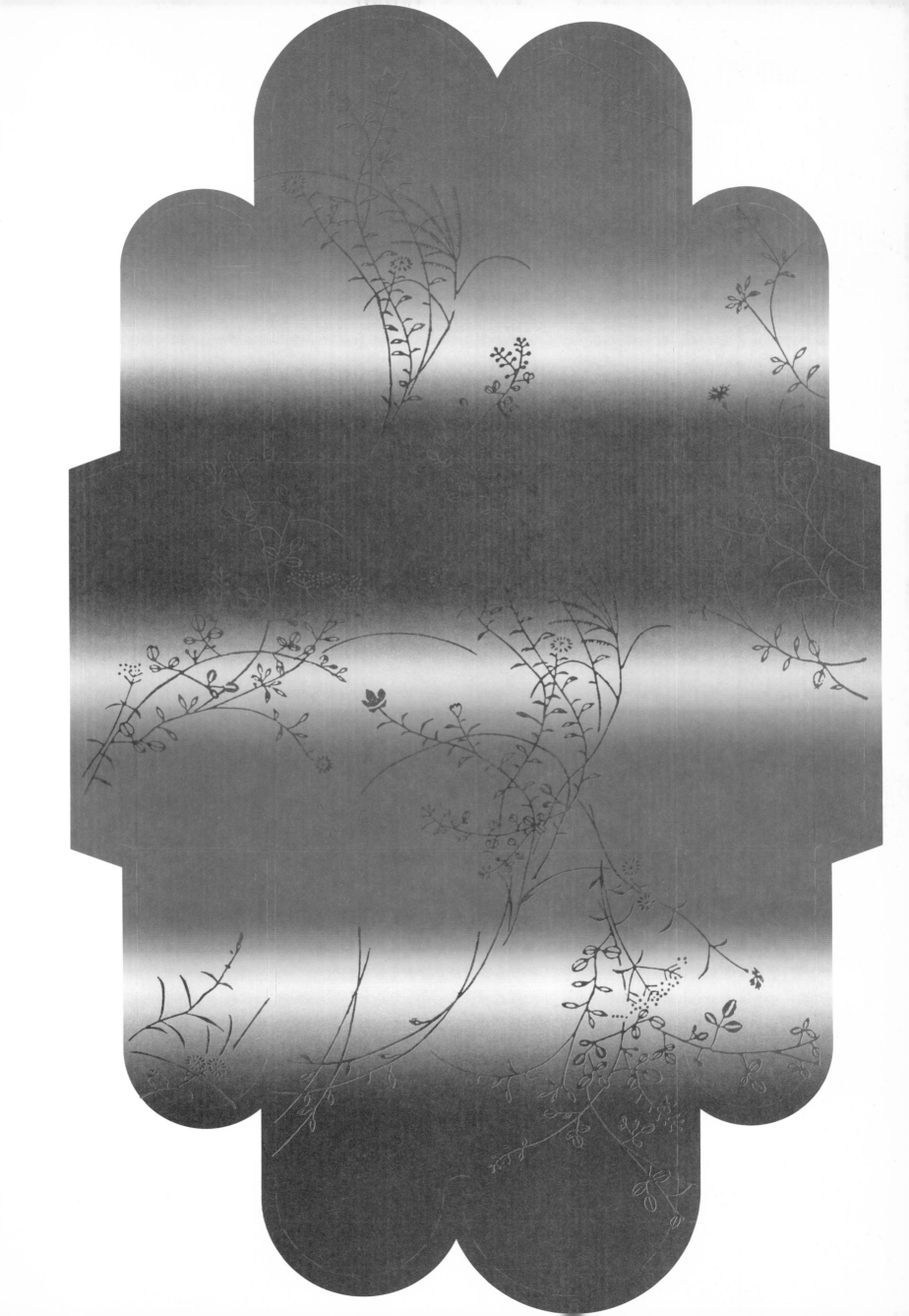

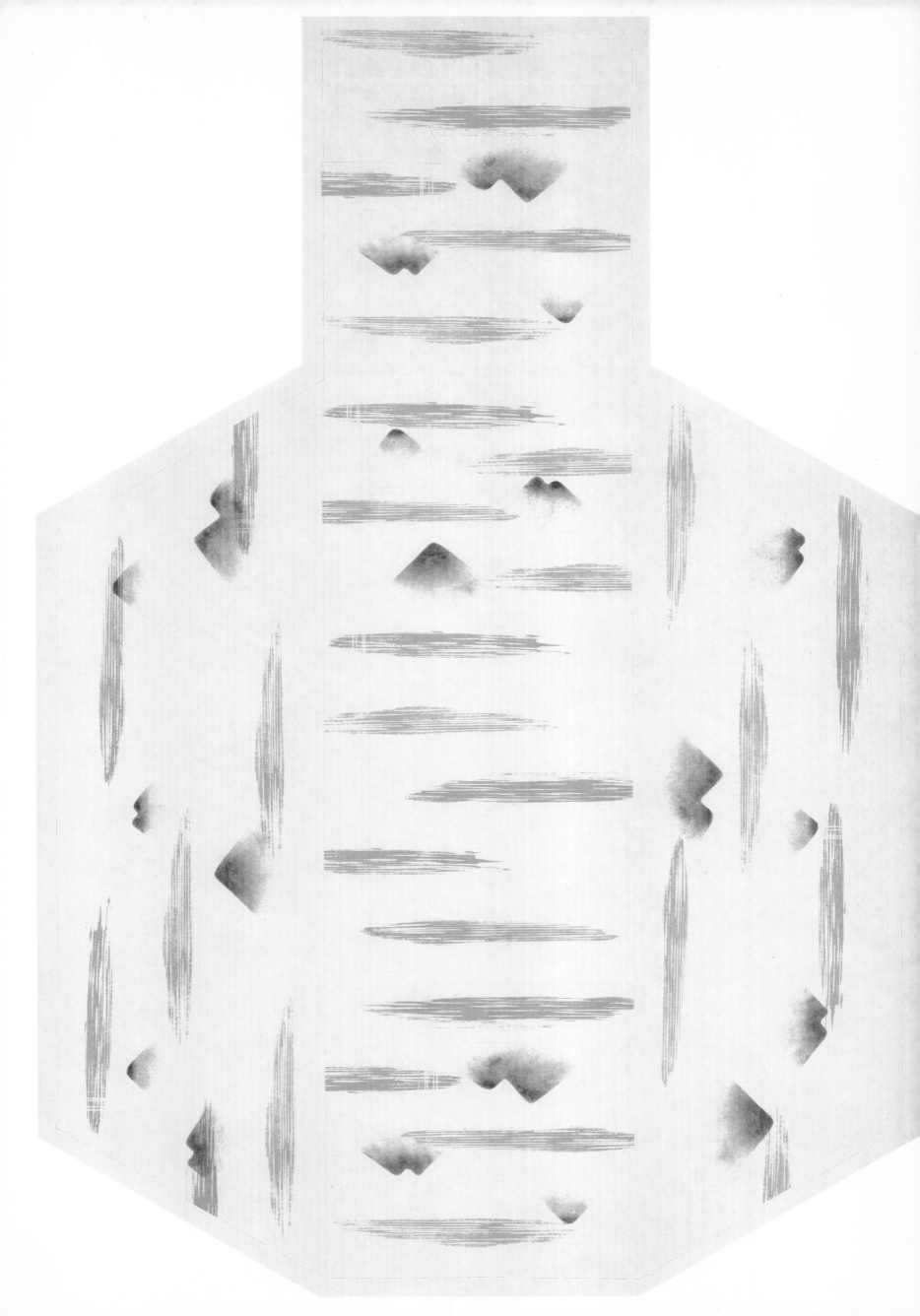

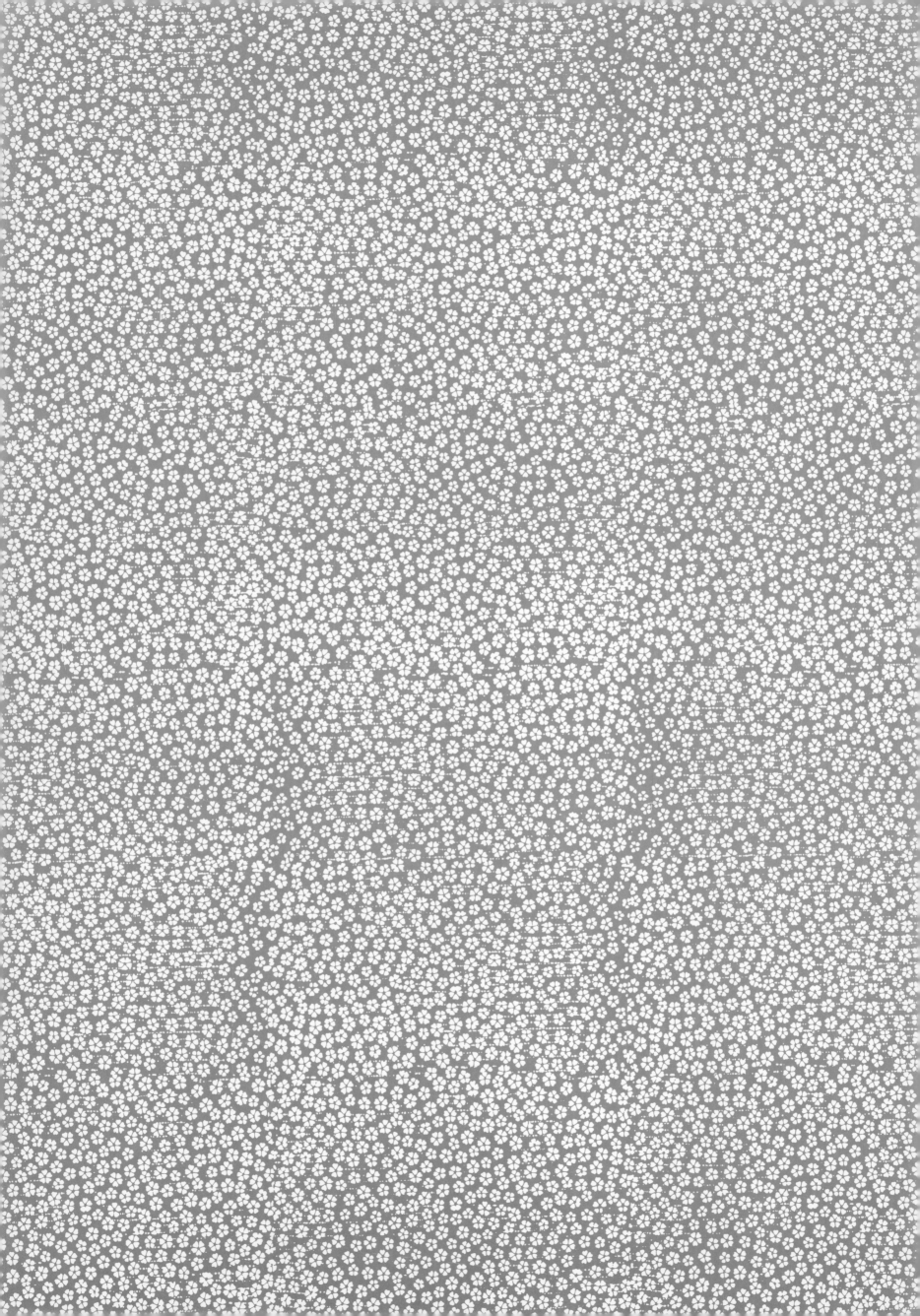

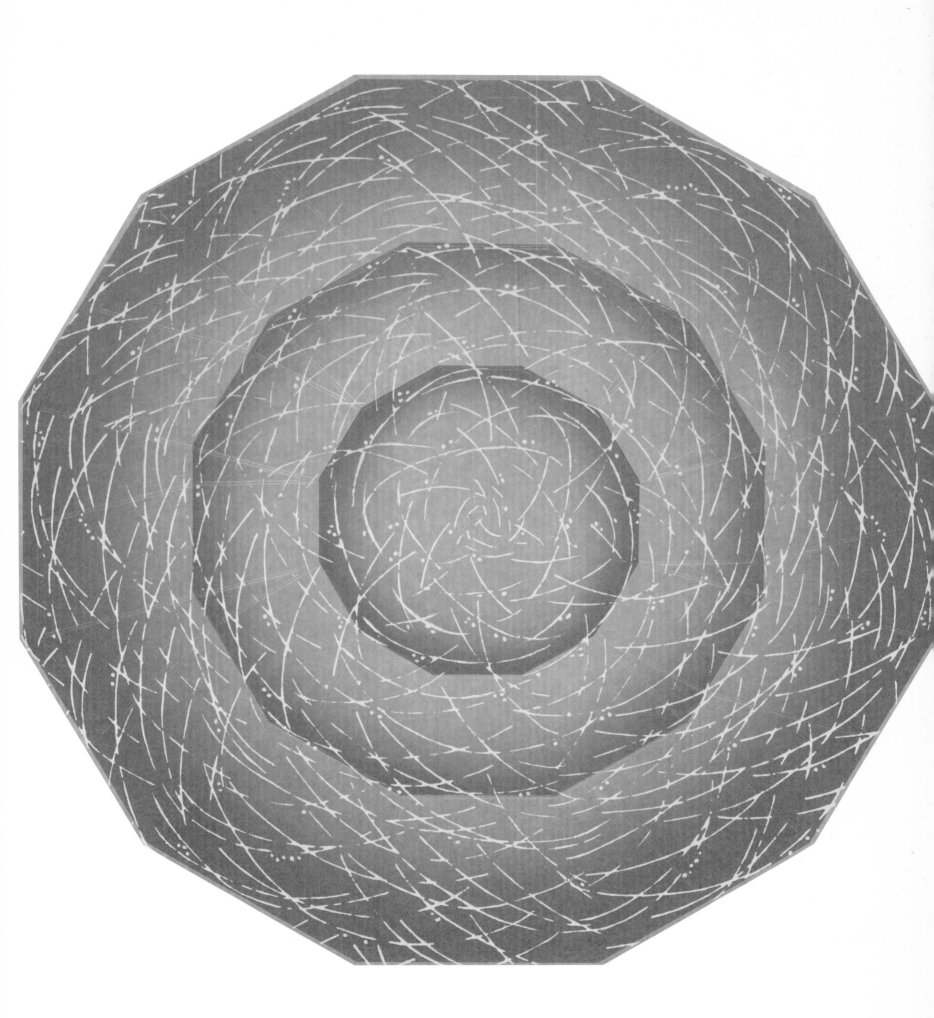

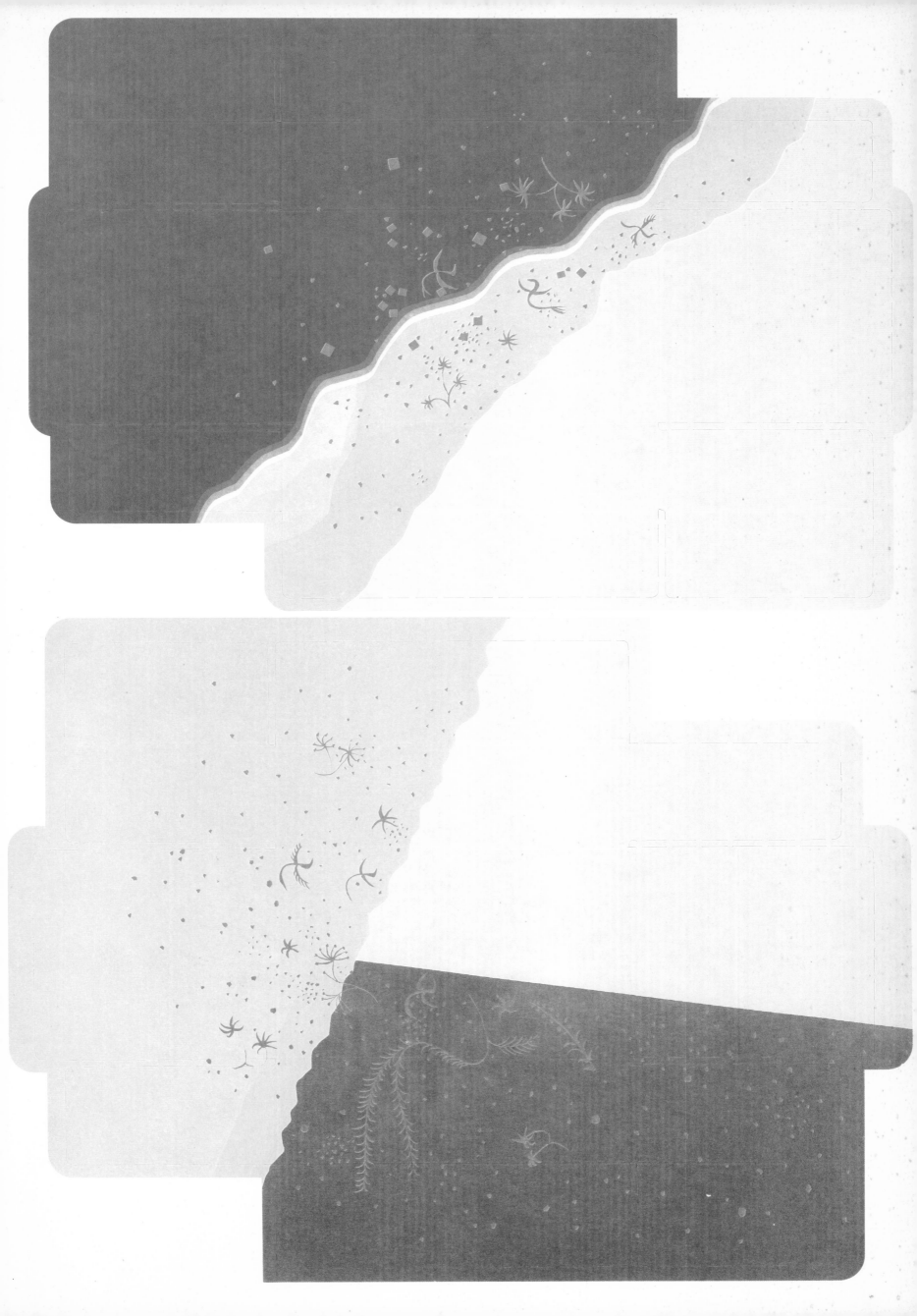